WAY GROSS SCIENCE™

THE GROSS SCIENCE OF
GERMS ALL AROUND YOU

CAROL HAND

rosen publishing's
rosen
central®

New York

Published in 2019 by The Rosen Publishing Group, Inc.
29 East 21st Street, New York, NY 10010

Library of Congress Cataloging-in-Publication Data

Names: Hand, Carol, 1945– author.
Title: The gross science of germs all around you / Carol Hand.
Description: New York : Rosen Central, 2019. | Series: Way gross science | Audience: Grades 5–8. | Includes bibliographical references and index.
Identifiers: LCCN 2017051541 | ISBN 9781508181682 (library bound) | ISBN 9781508181699 (paperback)
Subjects: LCSH: Microorganisms—Juvenile literature. | Bacteria—Juvenile literature. | Viruses—Juvenile literature.
Classification: LCC QR57 .H36 2019 | DDC 572/.42—dc23
LC record available at https://lccn.loc.gov/2017051541

Manufactured in the United States of America

CONTENTS

INTRODUCTION

Dr. Mark Sklansky is a germaphobe. When he touches a door or a computer keyboard, he knows he will contaminate his hands. That is, he will get germs or dirt on his hands. Then, he will transfer the germs or dirt to the next thing he touches. Dr. Sklansky works at the David Geffen School of Medicine at UCLA. As a doctor, he has to worry about germs.

Even though germs are everywhere, people are not in constant danger. How much people need to worry about germs depends on where they are. One place to worry is in hospitals. Anna Gorman, in an NPR article, reports that one of every twenty-five hospital patients get sick daily from an infection they got in the hospital. These infections often occur because hospital workers do not wash their hands. Almost all hospitals have strict handwashing rules. But only about 40 percent of hospital staff follow those rules.

Dr. Sklansky agrees that people need to follow the handwashing rules. But he uses another method to help limit the spread of germs even more. This is the handshake-free zone. In these parts of the hospital, people are discouraged from shaking hands. In 2015, Dr. Sklansky tried his method in the neonatal intensive care units (NICUs) at two UCLA hospitals. Doctors and nurses in these units care for premature or extremely sick babies. It is important that they do not get infections.

Dr. Sklansky explained to staff and families the reasons for not shaking hands. The method was presented not as a rule but as a suggestion. The hospital put up signs with diagrams showing a handshake with a line through it. The signs said, "To help reduce the spread of germs, our NICU is now a handshake-free zone. Please find other ways to greet

Handwashing is a basic sanitation procedure. Handwashing rules exist in every hospital. But sometimes hospital employees fail to follow the rules, and infections result.

each other." After a six-month trial period, people in the NICUs were used to not shaking hands. They greeted each other with a fist bump, wave, or bow.

Dr. Sklansky does not yet know if the rate of infections decreased in the NICUs when handshakes decreased. He is planning a future study to determine this. Another study showed that handshakes definitely transfer more germs than other greetings. The study measured the transfer of bacteria during handshakes, high

fives, and fist bumps. Handshakes transferred many bacteria. High-fives transferred only half as many. Fist bumps transferred only about 20 percent as many.

Maureen Shawn Kennedy, editor-in-chief of the *American Journal of Nursing*, thinks limiting handshakes in hospitals is an excellent idea. Kennedy says, "There are just so many reasons to avoid handshakes, even when people are washing their hands. Just because someone is walking around in a white coat...doesn't mean they don't have bacteria on their hands."

CHAPTER ONE

WHAT ARE GERMS?

Most people think germs are gross. But how many people really know what germs are? What do they look like? What do they do? Do all germs cause disease?

There are many kinds of germs. But all germs have one thing in common—they are microscopic. That is, they are so tiny they can only be seen through a microscope. Germs are also called microbes, or microorganisms. The prefix "micro" means "small." People who study microbes are called microbiologists.

KINDS OF GERMS

Most germs fall into one of two groups. They are either bacteria or viruses. Bacteria are tiny, single-celled organisms. They are much smaller than the cells in the human body. Most can be seen under a light microscope that magnifies them at least four hundred times. Bacterial cells are also simpler than human cells. Their genetic material (DNA) is not in a nucleus, but instead floats free inside the cell.

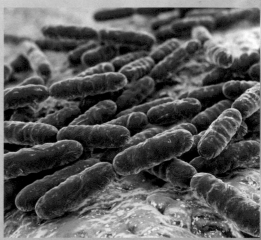

These highly magnified bacteria are *Lactobacillus*, which occur naturally in the human body, usually in the mouth and intestines.

WHAT BACTERIA LOOK LIKE

Bacteria are grouped into five different categories, based on the shape of their cells. Rod-shaped bacteria are called bacilli. *E. coli*, which lives in the human gut, and *Salmonella*, which causes food poisoning, are bacilli. Ball-shaped bacteria are called cocci. They include *Staphylococcus* and *Streptococcus*, which cause staph and strep infections. Vibrios are comma-shaped. The bacterium named *Vibrio* causes cholera. Spiral-shaped bacteria are called spirilla. One spirillum causes ulcers; another causes diarrhea in children. Finally, spirochetes are corkscrew-shaped. One type of spirochete causes Lyme disease. Sometimes, bacteria exist as single cells. In other cases, they occur in pairs, chains, or clusters.

Bacteria are enclosed by a cell wall. But bacteria are living cells. They get energy from the environment. They duplicate their DNA and reproduce by dividing in half to form two new cells.

Bacteria are found everywhere. They live in and on organisms, including people. They are found on surfaces, such as tables, doorknobs, and clothes. They live in air, water, and soil. Most bacteria are harmless, and many perform important functions in the world. Only a few types of bacteria are pathogens, or microbes that cause disease or infection. For example, bacteria cause ear infections, strep throat, and pneumonia.

Viruses are even smaller than bacteria. They can only be seen by a special microscope, called an electron microscope. It magnifies many times more than a light microscope. Viruses are not true cells. They are halfway between living and nonliving. They consist of pieces of genetic

WHAT VIRUSES LOOK LIKE

Like bacteria, viruses come in many shapes. The icosahedron is a rounded structure composed of twenty equilateral triangles fitted together. The rhinovirus, which causes the common cold, has an icosahedral shape. An icosahedral virus enclosed in a fatty layer is called an envelope virus. Influenza, or flu, viruses are this type. Helical viruses have a capsid shaped like a cylinder. Their genetic material is in the central cavity. Capsid proteins are arranged in a circle, forming the helix. The tobacco mosaic virus is helical. Finally, complex viruses have an icosahedral "head" and a helical "tail." They are called bacteriophages because they infect bacteria. Spider-like legs at the tail end attach to the bacterial cell.

material (either DNA or RNA) surrounded by a protective protein coat called a capsid. Unlike bacteria, viruses cannot take energy from the environment. They depend on a living cell or organism for both energy and reproduction. The cell or organism where they live and reproduce is the host.

As with bacteria, viruses are everywhere. They infect plants, animals, and bacteria. They are found on surfaces and everyday objects. Different viruses survive for different lengths of time outside living cells. Some die in seconds, others can live many years. All viruses are pathogens. Because they can only reproduce inside living cells, they must infect something to survive. This does not mean all viruses are dangerous or that all infect people. A virus that infects a frog, for example, would

Pregnant women infected by Zika often have children (such as these twins) with microcephaly, or abnormal brain development.

probably not survive in a human cell. Viruses cause colds and flu, chickenpox, rabies, and some cancers. They also cause deadly diseases such as Ebola, Zika, and HIV/AIDS.

A few other groups of germs, or microbes, also cause diseases. Protozoans, like bacteria, are single-celled organisms. *Amoeba* and *Paramecium* are examples. Protozoan cells are bigger and more like human cells. Like bacteria, only a few of them are pathogens. Many protozoans live in water and cause intestinal diseases. These diseases often cause pain and diarrhea. A few protozoans become parasites within the body and cause serious diseases. Some fungi (relatives of mushrooms) also cause diseases. Athlete's foot is a fungal disease.

HOW TINY ARE GERMS?

It is hard to imagine how tiny germs are. Bacteria are extremely small, and viruses are much smaller. To compare sizes, consider a meter in length. A meter equals thirty-nine inches (slightly longer than a yard, which is thirty-six inches). Sizes of bacteria and viruses are measured in nanometers, or billionths of a meter. Most bacteria range in size from 200 to 1,000 nanometers (nm). The largest known bacterium is barely visible to the naked eye. It is 75,000 nanometers (0.75 millimeter) in diameter.

Viruses range in size from about 20 to 750 nanometers. Forty-five thousand viruses of average size can fit across the width of a human hair.

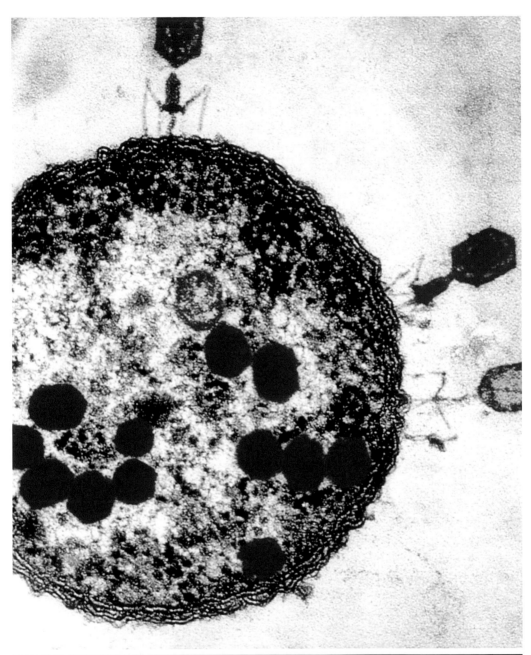

The large sphere in this highly magnified photo is an *E. coli* bacterium. It is being attacked by a number of bacteriophages, viruses that infect bacteria.

Dr. Donald Ganem, on the website BioInteractive, illustrated the relative sizes of microorganisms. If a human cell were approximately the size of an adult man, a typical bacterium would be the size of a football. A large virus would be about the size of a AA battery. A small virus would be the size of an aspirin.

ARE ALL GERMS BAD?

Bacteria are not just a vital part of air, water, and soil. They are also part of every living organism. For example, the human body contains ten times more bacterial cells than it does human cells. However, because bacterial cells are so tiny, all of them together weigh less than one-half pound (227 grams). Because people live with these bacterial cells every day, and usually stay healthy, it is obvious most bacteria are not dangerous.

No one knows for sure what percentage of bacteria are pathogens. That is because no one has counted all the types of bacteria. In an article on Phys.org, biology professor Michael Hadfield says, "The true number of bacterial species in the world is staggeringly huge." There are bacteria in the deep ocean, high in the atmosphere, in all land environments, and in and on every type of organism on Earth. Given this huge number, Hadfield concludes, "the proportion of all bacterial species that is pathogenic to plants and animals is surely small."

CHAPTER TWO

WHERE ARE GERMS FOUND?

The only germs people need to worry about are pathogens—germs that cause disease. But instead of worrying, why not find out where most of those germs are found? Why not learn how to avoid them, or how to clean areas where they are most likely to collect? In short, people can develop healthy habits. They can live with germs without getting sick.

HOW GERMS ARE SPREAD

People who understand how disease germs spread, and how to prevent their spread, will likely stay safe. Germs spread and expose people to diseases in four major ways.

First, germs spread by touching. A person touches something with disease germs on it. Then, the person touches their own body—eyes, nose, mouth, or a cut or scratch. The disease germs are transferred to that person's body. For example, Joe has recently acquired

Covering the mouth and nose is one of the most effective ways to lessen the spread of disease.

a flu virus. While talking near a staircase at school, Joe suddenly sneezes, spraying droplets of liquid into the air before he can cover his nose and mouth. Viral particles from the droplets settle on the staircase railing. A few minutes later, Susie arrives. As she starts up the stairs, she briefly grasps the railing. A small paper cut on her finger, received in her last class, is still open. Flu virus particles move from the railing to the cut on Susie's finger and into her bloodstream. Susie now has the flu virus.

Second, germs spread through breathing. Who was Joe talking to by the staircase? That person (and other people nearby) probably inhaled some viral particles just from being in the vicinity where Joe sneezed, even though he quickly covered his mouth and nose. Usually, in these situations, little harm is done. Few germs are spread because the contact is minimal. But suppose Joe did not try to cover his mouth and nose. Suppose no one covered their mouth when coughing. Many more germs would be spread if no one took precautions.

Third, germs spread through food and drink. Drinking water may be untreated or not treated properly. It carries disease germs, many of which cause diarrhea. Food that is not prepared properly may carry germs that people eat. Perhaps fruits and vegetables are not washed. Perhaps meats are not kept at the right temperature or are not completely cooked. The disease-causing organisms *E. coli* and *Salmonella* can be transmitted this way. Improperly canned foods can transmit the bacterium that causes botulism.

Fourth, animal bites from pets, wild animals, or insects can spread disease-causing germs. Even animals that do not look sick can carry pathogens. The most commonly known disease of this type is rabies, often caused by dog bites. But any mammal can carry rabies. According to the Washington State Department of Health, dogs bite about 4.5 million people in the United States every year. Children are most at risk. The bitten person should see a doctor so protective measures can be taken. Insect bites can also cause disease. Ticks carry Lyme disease. Fleas carry plague. Mosquitoes carry many diseases, including malaria and the Zika virus.

Disease germs can also spread by sexual contact, including kissing. A pregnant woman can spread disease germs to her unborn child. When drug users share needles, they run a high risk of transmitting disease. People can get disease germs from contaminated blood during a blood transfusion.

GERMS ON SURFACES

The organization NSF International looked at the number of germs on various surfaces in two elementary schools. They measured "colony-forming units" (CFUs), or the number of bacteria available to form colonies in each square inch of surface. By far the most bacteria (2.7 million CFU per square inch [6 square cm]) were found on classroom water fountain spigots. Only

Public water fountains have more germs than almost any other surface. This is why people should never touch their mouths or faces to the faucet when they drink.

CAN EXERCISE MAKE YOU SICK?

Linda Melone, writing for *Prevention* magazine, describes the grossest places in the typical gym or fitness center. These also apply to school gyms or locker rooms. Germs can easily hitch a ride on gym bags, which travel from place to place and often sit on the ground. Germs infect water bottles when they are opened, shared, or refilled. Flu germs are easily inhaled during crowded fitness classes. Steam rooms, especially floors and benches, often harbor fungi. Fitness balls, the seats and handlebars of spinning bikes, and kids' play areas transfer germs. Simple precautions, such as using disinfectant, can prevent most infections.

3,200 CFU were found on toilet seats. That is, water fountain spigots had more than 800 times as many germs as toilet seats. Other surfaces with many CFUs included cafeteria trays and plates, water faucet handles, and computer keyboards.

How long can germs live on surfaces? It depends on the germ. Some cold viruses can live on surfaces for several days, but their ability to cause colds declines rapidly. Most last less than twenty-four hours. On a person's hands, the cold-causing rhinovirus may stay infectious for at least an hour. Flu viruses usually survive on hard surfaces for twenty-four hours, but the amount present on a person's hands is very low after only five minutes. Flu viruses survive in air droplets for several hours, longer in cold air. Many bacteria that cause stomach bugs can survive for one to four hours on surfaces or fabrics. A few can survive much longer. The norovirus, which is transmitted through contaminated food and water, can survive for days to weeks; the bacterium *Clostridium dificile* up to five months.

GERMS AT HOME AND AWAY

Germs are everywhere in people's lives. In homes, the kitchen is the germiest place. The floor in front of the sink has the most germs. Dishwashing sponges have huge numbers. The sink can also harbor dangerous bacteria. If, for example, someone washes raw chicken in the sink, the sponges, faucets, and anything else within range can be contaminated with pathogens. In the bathroom, flushing the toilet with the seat up sprays toilet germs into the air. Sharing toothbrushes, makeup, and other personal items also transfers germs.

Many potentially dangerous microbes enter the house on the bottoms of shoes. According to Dr. Barry C. Fox, one study found nine different pathogenic bacteria in material on people's shoe soles. Removing shoes at the door can keep many germs out of the house. Electronic items are also great germ collectors. These include phones, pads, keyboards, and touchscreens. Sharing a phone or computer with a sick person is a sure way to transmit germs.

Outside the home, germs on technology are even more of a problem. Public computers or touchscreens, such as those in coffee shops or airports, transfer germs from strangers. In airports

Raw chicken often carries *Salmonella*, the bacterium responsible for most food poisoning. Be sure to disinfect everything and wash your hands after handling raw poultry.

or in bus or train terminals, or on the transports (airplanes, buses, trains), people have contact with strangers. This allows the spread of germs from distant places, to which local people may have no resistance. This is a major way epidemic and pandemic diseases spread. Restaurants—especially menus and salt and pepper shakers) transfer germs, too.

But wherever they are located, most germs are harmless. Practical, common-sense actions can prevent most infections.

MYTHS AND FACTS

Myth: All germs cause diseases.

Fact: Most germs are harmless and necessary for life. No one knows for sure what percentage of germs are harmful, because no one has yet identified all of them. According to the website Microbiology Online, the percentage of disease-causing bacteria and viruses is less than one percent. The other 99 percent are often helpful, for example, synthesizing vitamins, protecting the human body, and acting as decomposers and recyclers in the environment.

Myth: Antibiotics will cure a cold.

Fact: Colds are caused by viruses. Antibiotics kill only bacteria, not viruses. Antibiotics attack the bacterial cell wall or its ribosomes (protein-building structures), and have no effect on cold viruses, which lack these structures. Using antibiotics when they are not needed can contribute to antibiotic resistance, making antibiotics useless when they are needed.

Myth: Antibacterial wipes are the best way to clean hands.

Fact: Most experts agree that the best way to clean hands is to wash them with soap and water. Soap breaks down organic material and kills germs, and rinsing with water washes away most of the dirt and germs. Antibacterial wipes are the next best thing, if the hands are not visibly dirty. They do not remove organic material or dirt but they do kill most germs.

CHAPTER THREE

STAYING HEALTHY IN A GERMY WORLD

When people talk about the dangers of germs, they often use the words "infection" and "disease." Sometimes they talk as if these two words are the same. But they are not. An infection comes first. It occurs when a virus or bacterium enters a person's body from the environment and begins to multiply. This invasion, or infection, by a disease organism triggers the body's immune system to move into high gear. The body's disease-fighters, such as white blood cells and antibodies, begin to fight off the infection. They try to kill and remove the multiplying bacteria or viruses and prevent them from spreading further. This might take a few days. While it is happening, the person might cough or sneeze, or have a fever.

If the immune system cannot fight off the infection, it becomes a disease. A disease damages body cells and organs. It causes a set of signs and symptoms specific to each disease. For example, the *Anopheles* mosquito carries a protozoan parasite. A person bitten by a mosquito can become infected by the parasite. This infection causes the disease malaria. Sometimes, the process works the other way. A contagious disease can lead to infection of others. The pneumonia bacterium spreads through the air, so a person with pneumonia can spread it to those in the vicinity by coughing or just breathing.

Infection and disease differ in another way. Infections can be prevented by decreasing exposure to disease organisms. But they cannot be

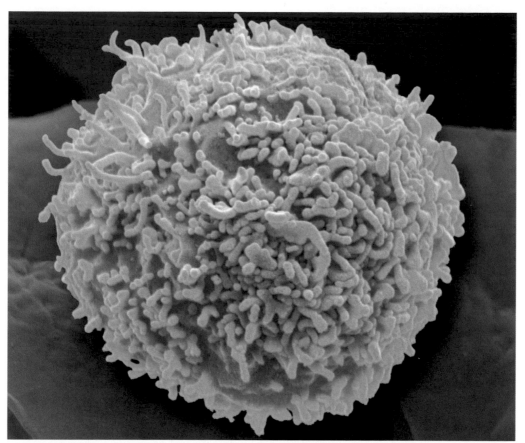

This lymphocyte, a type of white blood cell, is an essential part of the human immune system. Some lymphocytes make antibodies; others kill cancer cells or cells infected by viruses.

cured, because they depend on organisms in the environment. Diseases can be treated and cured with medications. Thus, the best way to avoid getting a disease is to prevent getting an infection.

PERSONAL HYGIENE

According to the Mayo Clinic, one of the easiest and best ways to prevent infection is handwashing. Although often overlooked, handwashing is extremely effective. Hands should always be washed after coughing or sneezing, using the bathroom, or changing a diaper. They should be washed before and after preparing food, before inserting or removing contact lenses, and before treating wounds, giving medicines, or touching sick or injured people. In families with pets, hands should be washed after playing with pets or handling pet waste. Soap and water are best, but hand-sanitizing gels made with alcohol are also good.

Personal hygiene also includes covering the nose and mouth when a person coughs or sneezes. According to Dr. Barry C. Fox, germs from a cough or sneeze can travel 6 to 8 feet (1.8 to 2.4 meters). The best way to prevent this is to cough or sneeze into the crook of the elbow, not into the hand. A person normally touches his or her face up to twenty times per hour. Far fewer germs are spread if the person does not touch the eyes, nose, or mouth.

What about the five-second rule, which says it is OK to eat something dropped on the floor if it is picked up within five seconds? This

HANDWASHING 101

To wash hands with soap and water, lather hands fully with soap, covering all sides and fingers. Rub hands together (including all sides and fingers, under fingernails, and wrists) for a full twenty-four seconds. This is the time it takes to sing "Happy Birthday" twice. This might seem like a long time, but it is the best way to remove most germs and prevent infections. Using an alcohol hand gel is similar. Put the gel in the palm of one hand. Apply enough to wet both hands completely. Rub the hands together, cleaning all parts (including fingers, nails, and wrists) until they are dry. This should take twenty-five to thirty seconds. People should always wash their hands carefully to stay healthy.

is probably fine most of the time, according to Dr. Fox. But he also reported that scientists at Clemson University did a study in which they applied *Salmonella* bacteria to tile, wood, and carpet. They found that, within five seconds, bread and bologna dropped onto the surfaces picked up hundreds to thousands of *Salmonella* germs.

KEEPING SURFACES CLEAN

It is important to keep surfaces that people touch often relatively clean. This is done with disinfectants. Chlorine bleach, a common disinfectant, kills about 99 percent of pathogens, according to Dr. Fox. Vinegar is a natural product. It appears to kill about 80 percent of viruses and 90 percent of bacteria, according to Fox. It kills flu viruses, but not *Staphylococcus* (staph) bacteria. The Environmental Protection Agency (EPA) has a list of environmentally responsible cleaning agents. In addition

GOOD TEEN HYGIENE

The hormones and body changes resulting from puberty also change hygiene needs. Teens who practice several basic hygiene activities will be clean and pleasant to be around, and will avoid infections. A daily shower using a mild soap is a must. If a person's hair is oily, it can be washed every day. If it is dry, a day or two can be skipped. To prevent acne, the face can be washed (gently) twice a day. Use deodorant or antiperspirant daily. Wear clean clothes, especially underwear, every day. Brush and floss teeth daily. Maintaining good oral health prevents both tooth decay and bad breath. It is especially important if the person is drinking acidic or sugary drinks, such as coffee or soda.

to vinegar, the list includes thymol, made from the herb thyme. Thymol is found in many cleaning agents. Tea tree oil, an organic product, helps destroy MRSA, a type of staph infection that has become resistant to many antibiotics.

Many disinfectant products are available as sprays or wipes. Since it is more difficult to know how clean surfaces are in public places, many people carry small sprays or packets of wipes. These can be used to clean surfaces in restaurants, public restrooms, transportation, elevators, or other public places. Keeping a few on hand, in your pocket, purse, or glove compartment of your car, where they can be accessed quickly, is a smart idea.

The aromatic herb thyme, shown here, is commonly used as a flavor in cooking. Its ingredient, thymol, has disinfectant properties and is used in many cleaning products.

In everyday life, germs are handled by disinfection, which gets rid of most, but not all, microorganisms on surfaces. Disinfection makes viruses inactive. It does not kill spores, or resting stages, of some microbes. In special cases, sterilization is needed. Sterilization kills all microbes. It is done during surgery and in certain parts of laboratories, industrial processes, and hospitals. Heating or steam, ultraviolet radiation, high pressure, filtration, or certain chemicals are used to sterilize surfaces and objects.

Generally, being aware of where disease-causing germs may lurk and using common-sense precautions, such as handwashing, can keep a person healthy. There is no need to freak out over germs, even though they might be gross.

CHAPTER FOUR

GERMS AND DISEASES

Pathogens only cause disease when they overwhelm the body's immune system. There are so many germs, or the germs are so virulent (strong and harmful), that the immune system can't work fast enough to stop them.

Viruses cause disease by killing cells or disrupting their functions. Different viruses invade distinct types of cells. Cold and flu viruses enter respiratory or intestinal cells. HIV invades immune system cells. But once inside the cell, all viral particles act the same way. They take over the cell's machinery. They reproduce using their own genetic material and make proteins using the cell's materials. They fill up the cell with new viral particles. The cell eventually bursts and the particles enter new cells, spreading the infection.

Bacteria also kill cells and disrupt their functions. But they reproduce on their own, instead of using the host cells' materials and structures. They can multiply very rapidly, crowding out and destroying host cells and tissues. They kill some cells and tissues outright. They may make toxins that paralyze cells, destroy their functions, or cause a toxic immune reaction.

HOW DOCTORS FIGHT DISEASES

Most disease organisms never enter the body. The skin, membranes in the nose and throat, and other surface structures are the body's first line of defense. They trap and prevent microbes from entering. Once an infection occurs, the microbes activate the immune system. White blood cells rush to the infection site to kill the invaders. Antibodies, special proteins that recognize the pathogen, begin to multiply and help white blood cells. When the immune system turns on, the person may have a fever. Tissue around an infection site becomes inflamed and may fill with pus. This means the immune system is working. If it successfully kills off invading cells, the symptoms go away in a few days.

If the infection becomes a disease, sometimes people treat it with over-the-counter (OTC) medicines. OTCs do not require a doctor's prescription. Some treat symptoms such as itching, pain, or coughs. Some cure diseases, such as athlete's foot. Some treat problems that come back often, such as migraines. A person with a cold might take an OTC cold remedy. This does not cure the cold, but it controls cold symptoms. It makes the person comfortable while the body's immune system removes the virus.

But if a disease is serious, or OTC remedies do not work, the next step is to visit a doctor. Doctors try to determine the exact cause of the disease and prescribe a specific drug to fight it. For bacterial infections, this is an antibiotic. Antibiotics either kill bacteria outright or inhibit bacterial growth. There are many different antibiotics. Some target the bacterial cell wall or cell membrane. Others target enzymes that control bacterial processes. Some come from natural sources (such as penicillin, which is made from a mold). Others are synthetic (made in a laboratory).

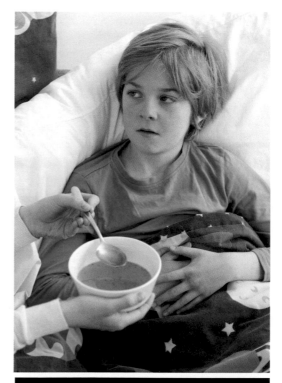

For minor illnesses, such as colds and flu, doctors often prescribe rest, healthy food, and plenty of fluids, including Mom's chicken soup.

Some antibiotics target and kill many different bacteria. These broad-spectrum antibiotics include penicillin, tetracycline, and cephalosporin. Doctors may prescribe them when they are not sure which bacterium is causing an infection. Other antibiotics target a specific type or a small group of bacteria. They are used when the disease-causing bacterium is known. For example, erythromycin is used to treat bacterial pneumonia and several strep infections.

Bacterial and viral infections may have similar symptoms (coughing, sneezing, fever, inflammation, vomiting, diarrhea, and fatigue). Some diseases (for example, pneumonia) can be caused by either a virus or a bacterium. However, they cannot be treated with the same drugs. Antibiotics do not work on viruses. Antiviral medicines have been developed for some viral diseases, for example, HIV/AIDS and herpes simplex. But for minor viral diseases, such as colds and flu, the best advice is to rest, eat properly, and drink plenty of fluids. This allows

WHY ANTIBIOTICS DON'T WORK ON VIRUSES

Different antibiotics work in different ways. Some attack bacterial cell walls. They may interfere with the building of the cell wall and weaken it. Or they may make holes in an existing cell wall. In either case, antibodies and immune cells can then enter the bacterial cell and kill it. Other antibiotics act on the bacteria's ribosomes, structures necessary to build proteins. If ribosomes cannot function properly, the bacterial cell cannot repair itself or make new materials. But viruses are simply genetic material surrounded by a protein coat. They lack both cell walls and ribosomes. There is nothing in the viral structure for the antibiotic to attack, so it has no effect on viruses.

the body's immune system time to mobilize and control the infection causing the disease.

PREVENTING DISEASES

Most people would agree it is better not to get a disease in the first place. People can prevent many diseases by taking vaccines. Vaccines are killed or weakened disease organisms, or parts of these organisms. They are usually injected and produce immunity to the disease. Because the disease organism is killed or weakened, vaccines are safe. Once inside the body, they cause the body to recognize the disease. The next time the

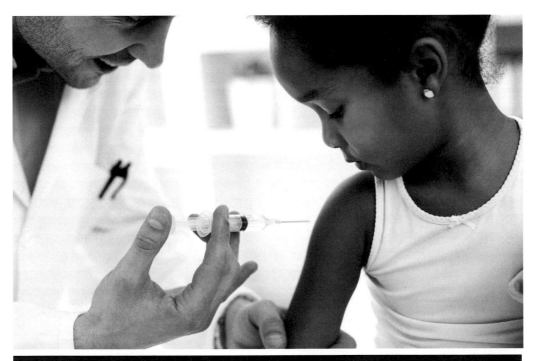

Since the early 1900s, vaccines have become a common (and now mandatory) way to prevent serious diseases. Vaccines produce disease immunity 90 to 100 percent of the time.

body is exposed to the disease microbe, it will quickly produce antibodies to fight that disease. Even if attacked by the disease organism, vaccinated people will not get sick.

Babies and young children receive many vaccines. By the age of five, those who receive a full set of vaccines are protected from many diseases, including measles, polio, tetanus, diphtheria, and whooping cough. Vaccines have nearly eliminated smallpox, polio, and many other diseases around the world.

HOW CLEAN IS TOO CLEAN?

A theory called the hygiene hypothesis suggests that people sometimes go too far in protecting their children from germs. This hypothesis says that, if children are not exposed to ordinary germs, their immune

Elementary school children receive a spritz of hand sanitizer as they line up for lunch. These teachers are battling a swine flu epidemic in the area.

systems will not develop properly. Then, when they encounter these germs later in life, they will not be able to deal with them. This leads to more immune-related diseases, such as asthma and allergies. In an article on Health & Wellness, Dr. Marie-Claire Arrieta of Canada's University of Alberta points out that most microbes are not harmful. In fact, most are helpful, especially when kids are young. "To think having dirt on you can make you sick is a misunderstanding," she says.

When children are in contact with germs, their immune systems are stimulated to produce more immune cells. Delays in exposure weaken the immune system. Also, too much cleanliness prevents kids from developing necessary colonies of intestinal bacteria. Scientists such as Dr. Arrieta suggest simply letting kids grow normally. That is, do not deliberately expose them to dangerous microbes. But also, do not try to protect them from everyday germs. For example, do not feed them sterile foods, constantly disinfect their toys, or prevent them from playing outside or with other children. For both children and adults, a healthy immune system combined with sensible hygiene habits are all the protection needed from most microbes. Serious infectious diseases can be handled with medicines or, ideally, by protective vaccinations received in childhood.

CHAPTER FIVE

TO KILL OR NOT TO KILL

A re germs really gross? Or have people been taught to fear germs when they really don't need to? The answer is probably both. Some germs are dangerous and contagious. Throughout human history, pathogens have caused pandemics that killed millions of people. Germs caused bubonic plague, typhoid fever, malaria, smallpox, HIV/AIDS, Ebola, tetanus, pneumonia, and the Spanish flu of 1918.

But dangerous germs are far from the whole story. Very few microbes are dangerous. Bacteria live in and on the human body (and in and on every other organism). They live in and on everything on Earth. According to *The Encyclopedia of Earth*, there are 50 million bacteria in a single gram (0.035 ounce) of soil. The biomass of bacteria on Earth is greater than the biomass of all its plants and animals combined, and most bacteria have not even been described.

WHEN NOT TO KILL GERMS

Good bacteria in the human intestine have many functions. They help break down food. They produce vitamins and other substances used by the body. They strengthen the immune system and protect the body from pathogens. In nature, bacteria are decomposers in all food webs. They break down and

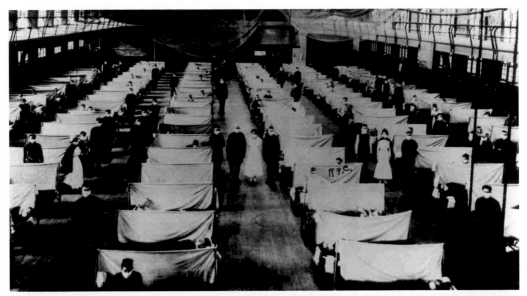

Millions of people died in the 1918 influenza epidemic. Here, a warehouse is converted to form a makeshift quarantine facility, as people try to limit the spread of the epidemic.

recycle nutrients. Without bacteria, dead matter would pile up, organisms would have no food, and ecosystems would die. Bacteria carry out nitrogen fixation. They trap nitrogen from the atmosphere, providing food for plants. Bacteria break down toxic compounds in soil, waste water, and pollution, such as oil spills. Most bacteria are essential to life on Earth. They need to be appreciated and protected, not destroyed.

A few people interpret the hygiene hypothesis to mean hygiene isn't necessary. This is not the case. Good hygiene habits—washing hands and brushing teeth, for example—are always important to prevent the spread of pathogens. But this does not mean sterilizing homes (that is impossible, anyway) or being obsessively clean. It does not mean being dirt free. It means stopping germs in places and situations where they are most likely to spread. This includes places where food is prepared, in bathrooms, and around sick and infected people.

Developing a routine of good hygiene habits, including brushing one's teeth, is essential to preventing infections. But sterilization or constant disinfection is not necessary because most germs are harmless.

To stay healthy, people should have a balance of exposure to good and bad germs in the environment. This helps the body learn to deal with harmful germs. It keeps the body supplied with the helpful germs it needs to function properly. Thus, going outdoors and getting dirty is fine—even healthy. But in appropriate situations, hygiene habits are healthy, too. In short, it is important to understand that germs can be both good and bad, and to know where the bad ones lurk. It is important to live comfortably with germs, instead of assuming all of them are gross.

ANTIBIOTIC RESISTANCE AND SUPERBUGS

Advertisers often say cleaning products "kill 99 percent of all germs." This sounds like a good thing. But it is the starting point for one of the most

HOW BACTERIA BECOME SUPERBUGS

An antibiotic (or a cleaner) kills off most, but not all, of the bacteria it targets. The bacteria that survive (perhaps only 1 percent of them) are those most resistant to that antibiotic. They are also the only ones left to reproduce the next generation of bacteria. Thus, all bacteria in Generation 2 are far more resistant than those in Generation 1. Next time, doctors use a stronger antibiotic. Perhaps it kills off 90 percent of the second generation. The remaining ten percent are again the most resistant. When they reproduce to form Generation 3, it is far more resistant than Generation 2. It takes very few generations to produce "superbugs" or "super bacteria" that are unfazed by most antibiotics.

serious disease problems of the twenty-first century. That problem is antimicrobial resistance, or antibiotic resistance. This simply means that bacteria are becoming more resistant to the antibiotics used to treat them. It takes higher doses of antibiotics, or stronger types of antibiotics, to kill off an infecting bacterium. It becomes a superbug.

In February 2017, the World Health Organization (WHO) released a list of a dozen superbugs that pose serious threats to human health. Many public health experts consider these superbugs just as dangerous as new viruses such as Ebola and Zika. If antibiotics no longer kill them, doctors have no way to stop their spread or treat the diseases they cause. Many people with these diseases will die, especially members of vulnerable populations. These include young children, the elderly, and people with damaged immune systems, such as cancer patients.

The main reason superbugs are increasing is overuse of antibiotics. According to the Centers for Disease Control and Prevention (CDC), only half of antibiotics are prescribed properly. The wrong dosage may be prescribed, or they may be prescribed when not needed (for example, when the infection is viral, not bacterial). Antibiotics are given routinely to livestock animals, which later become human food. These antibiotics are used to promote growth, not to treat infections. Finally, resistant strains of bacteria and fungi can spread from person to person, and from animals to people. As of 2017, the CDC estimated more than two million illnesses and 23,000 deaths per year were due to antibiotic-resistant bacteria and fungi.

The CDC recommends four ways to decrease antibiotic resistance. First, prevent infections, which decreases the need for antibiotics. The WHO points out that vaccination is highly effective in preventing disease and reducing antibiotic resistance. Second, tracking information on antibiotic-resistant infections helps develop effective ways to fight them. Third, researchers must continue to develop new antibiotics. This is necessary because, although antibiotic resistance can be slowed, it cannot be stopped. Finally, doctors (and farmers) need to stop overuse and incorrect use of antibiotics. According to the CDC, this the most important control method.

Antibiotic resistance is one way an excess concern with germs can cause problems. The best approach is to realize that, yes, germs can be dangerous. Some do cause serious diseases and should be avoided. But gross or not, all germs are important, and most are helpful, even essential, to life. All microbes—bacteria, viruses, fungi, and protozoans—should be respected.

Antibiotics, such as amoxicillin, are important in controlling bacterial infections. But too much use of antibiotics can lead to antibiotic resistance.

10 GREAT QUESTIONS TO ASK
A MICROBIOLOGIST

1. What are germs? Do all germs cause diseases? What is a pathogen?
2. What is the difference between bacteria and viruses?
3. How do germs spread from place to place?
4. What places, surfaces, or objects have the most germs?
5. What is the difference between infection and disease?
6. What are the best ways to prevent the spread of pathogens?
7. What is the difference between disinfection and sterilization? When is each used?
8. What is the hygiene hypothesis, and how does it relate to being safe from germs?
9. How do antibiotics and vaccines fight pathogens? How are they different?
10. What is antibiotic resistance, what causes it, and why is it a problem?

GLOSSARY

antibiotic A type of medicine that kills bacteria or inhibits their growth; antibiotics have no effect on viruses.

antibiotic resistance (antimicrobial resistance) The ability of microbes (bacteria) to resist the effects of antibiotics due to overuse of the antibiotics; this makes the microbes more dangerous because the antibiotic no longer kills them or inhibits their growth.

antibodies Special proteins made by cells in the immune system; they recognize and attack specific disease microbes, allowing a rapid immune response when the microbe enters the body.

bacteria (single: bacterium) Members of a large group of single-celled microorganisms; a few cause diseases, but most are harmless and have important functions in the body and environment.

contagious (infectious) Relates to spread of an infection; when a disease organism spreads from person to person by direct or indirect contact (for example, by sneezing or coughing).

contaminate To make something impure or unclean by exposing it to dirt or pollution, or infecting it with germs.

disinfect To remove most of the disease agents from an area or surface, so the area is safe from infection or disease; unlike sterilization, disinfection does not remove all life forms.

epidemic An outbreak of a disease, for example, influenza, that spreads over a wide area such as a community or region.

hygiene Conditions and practice that prevent disease by keeping a person clean; washing hands and brushing teeth are examples.

hygiene hypothesis The theory that, if a young child's environment is too clean (if the child is protected from exposure to normal germs), the child's immune system will not develop properly, resulting in more infections (for example, allergies or asthma) later in life.

immune system The system in the human body that protects against disease; it includes special chemicals (such as antibodies), cells (such as white blood cells), tissues (such as lymph tissue and bone marrow), and organs (such as the thymus gland).

infection The invasion of germs such as bacteria or viruses into the body, where they reproduce; this triggers the actions of the immune system and is the first step in the disease process.

microbe (also microorganism) A very tiny, microscopic organism or germ, such as a bacterium or virus.

microbiologist A scientist who studies microbes, or microorganisms.

over-the-counter drug (OTC drug) A drug bought from a pharmacy without a prescription to treat or cure minor diseases, giving the immune system time to work.

pandemic An outbreak of a disease that is more widespread than an epidemic, usually covering a whole country or more than one country.

pathogen A microbe (usually a bacterium or virus) that causes disease or infection.

sterilize To remove, kill, or deactivate all life forms, especially microbes, in or on an area or surface.

superbug A slang term for a bacterium that has become very resistant to the antibiotics used to treat it; because it is drug-resistant, a superbug is dangerous, even deadly.

toxin A poison made by a living organism, especially a microorganism, that causes disease; many bacteria cause disease by producing low concentrations of toxins in host cells.

vaccine An agent made from a weakened form of a disease-causing microbe; when taken into the body, it protects the person from the disease by causing the person to make antibodies against it.

virulent Having extremely severe or harmful effects; used to describe certain disease organisms (bacteria or viruses).

virus A structure composed of a piece of genetic information (DNA or RNA) enclosed in a protein coat; it is structurally simpler than a living cell and must infect a living cell to feed and reproduce; viruses cause many diseases.

FOR MORE INFORMATION

Centers for Disease Control and Prevention (CDC)
1600 Clifton Road
Atlanta, GA 30329-4027
(800) CDC-INFO or (800) 232-4636
Website: https://www.cdc.gov
Facebook: @CDC
Twitter: @CDCgov
Instagram: cdcgov
The CDC is the primary agency concerned with disease threats for all
    US citizens, at home and abroad. Its website is filled with information
    on diseases and security of all kinds, including diseases and conditions,
    healthy living, environmental health, and emergency preparedness.

IPAC (Infection Prevention and Control Canada)
PO Box 46125 RPO Westdale
Winnipeg MB R3R 3S3
Canada
(866) 999-7111
Website: https://ipac-canada.org/index.php
Facebook and Twitter: @IPACCanada
This Canadian nonprofit organization is for anyone involved in infection-
    control activities. Its website contains a thorough discussion of various
    infectious diseases, hand hygiene, and antibiotic-resistant organisms,
    plus links for further education.

Mayo Clinic
200 First Street SW
Rochester, MN 55905
(507) 284-2511
Website: http://www.mayoclinic.org/patient-care-and-health-information
Facebook and Twitter: @MayoClinic
Instagram: mayoclinic

The Mayo Clinic website has considerable information on various diseases, including infectious diseases, as well as their symptoms, tests required to diagnose them, and drugs used to treat them.

Teens, Meet Vaccines
Public Health Agency of Canada
130 Colonnade Road
A.L. 6501H
Ottawa, ON K1A 0K9
Canada
(844) 280-5020
Website: https://www.canada.ca/en/public-health
Twitter: @CPHO_Canada
This website, sponsored by the Canadian Government's Public Health Agency, gives basic but thorough information on what vaccines are, how they work, and why they are important.

US Food and Drug Administration (FDA)
10903 New Hampshire Avenue
Silver Spring, MD 20993
1-888-INFO-FDA (1-888-463-6332)
Website: https://www.fda.gov
Facebook: @FDA
Twitter: @US_FDA
Instagram: us_fda
The FDA is the US agency that monitors food and drug safety. It determines if food is safe from germs and if drugs (including vaccines) are safe and effective for their given uses.

FOR FURTHER READING

Baby Professor. *Virus vs. Bacteria. Knowing the Difference* (Biology 6th Grade, Children's Biology Books). Seattle, WA: Amazon.com, 2017.

Baum, Margaux. *Bacteria*. (Germs: Disease-Causing Organisms). New York, NY: Rosen Publishing, 2017.

Baum, Margaux. *The Fight Against Germs* (Germs: Disease-Causing Organisms). New York, NY: Rosen Publishing, 2017.

Baum, Margaux. *Viruses* (Germs: Disease-Causing Organisms). New York, NY: Rosen Publishing, 2017.

Faulk, Michelle, PhD. *The Case of the Flesh-Eating Bacteria. Annie Biotica Solves Skin Disease Crimes* (Body System Disease Investigations). New York, NY: Enslow Publishing, 2013.

Kelly, Evelyn B., PhD, Ian Wilker, and Marylou Ambrose. *Tuberculosis and Superbugs. Examining TB and Bacterial Infections* (Diseases, Disorders, Symptoms). New York, NY: Enslow Publishing, 2014.

Miles, Amanda. *Cell Wars. In the Beginning*. Seattle, WA: CreateSpace Independent Publishing Platform (An Amazon Company), 2014.

Miles, Amanda. *Cell Wars II: Virus Invasion* (Volume 2). Seattle, WA: CreateSpace Independent Publishing Platform (An Amazon Company), 2015.

Reichs, Kathy, and Brendan Reichs. *Code: A Virals Novel*. New York, NY: Puffin Books (Penguin Random House), 2013.

Reichs, Kathy, and Brendan Reichs. *Exposure: A Virals Novel*. New York, NY: Puffin Books (Penguin Random House), 2015.

Reichs, Kathy, and Brendan Reichs. *Seizure* (Virals, Book 2). New York, NY: Puffin Books (Penguin Random House), 2013.

Reichs, Kathy, and Brendan Reichs. *Terminal: A Virals Novel*. New York, NY: Puffin Books (Penguin Random House), 2016.

Reichs, Kathy, and Brendan Reichs. *Virals* (Virals, Book 1). New York, NY: Puffin Books (Penguin Random House), 2011.

Simons, Rae. *A Kids' Guide to Viruses and Bacteria* (Understanding Disease and Wellness: Kids' Guides to Why People Get Sick and How They Can Stay Well) (Volume 13). Vestal, NY: Village Earth Press, 2016.

BIBLIOGRAPHY

Aron. "Difference Between Infection and Disease." DifferenceBetween.com, May 27, 2011. http://www.differencebetween.com /difference-between-infection-and-vs-disease.

Bailey, Regina. "Differences Between Bacteria and Viruses." ThoughtCo, August 18, 2016. https://www.thoughtco.com /differences-between-bacteria-and-viruses-4070311.

BioInteractive. "Size Analogies of Bacteria and Viruses." hhmi, 2000 and Beyond: Confronting the Microbe Menace, 2017. http://www.hhmi .org/biointeractive/size-analogies-bacteria-and-viruses.

CDC. "About Antimicrobial Resistance." Centers for Disease Control and Prevention, September 19, 2017. https://www.cdc.gov /drugresistance/about.html.

Communicable Disease Control and Prevention. "Germs." San Francisco Department of Public Health, 2017. http://www.sfcdcp.org/germs.html.

Davis, Charles P., MD, PhD. "The Hygiene Hypothesis." Medicine Net, 2017. http://www.medicinenet.com/script/main/art .asp?articlekey=155757.

Diffen. "Disinfect vs. Sterilize." Retrieved August 1, 2017. http://www .diffen.com/difference/Disinfect_vs_Sterilize.

Dworkin, Dr. Barry. "Microbiology 101: Why Antibiotics Don't Kill Viruses." *Ottawa Citizen*, January 28, 2003. http://www .drbarrydworkin.com/articles/medicine/infectious-disease-articles /microbiology-101-why-antibiotics-dont-kill-viruses.

The Encyclopedia of Earth. "Bacteria." December 29, 2016. https:// editors.eol.org/eoearth/wiki/Bacteria.

Fox, Barry C., MD. "Germ Are All Around Us: How Can We Stay Healthy?" The Great Courses Daily, The Teaching Company, LLC, Retrieved August 1, 2017. https://www.thegreatcoursesdaily.com /germs-around-us.

Freudenrich, Craig, PhD. "How Viruses Work." HowStuffWorks.com, October 19, 2000. http://science.howstuffworks.com/life /cellular-microscopic/virus-human.htm.

Fuhrman, Joel H. "What Are the Functions of Good Bacteria?" Sharecare, 2010–2017, Retrieved October 16, 2017. https://www.sharecare.com/health/bacterial-infections/what-functions-good-bacteria.

Gorman, Anna. "Handshake-Free Zones Target Spread of Germs in the Hospital." NPR, May 29, 2017. http://www.npr.org/sections/health-shots/2017/05/29/529878742/handshake-free-zones-target-spread-of-germs-in-the-hospital.

Griffin, R. Morgan. "Teen Hygiene Tips." Web MD, 2010. http://www.webmd.com/parenting/features/teen-hygiene#1.

Kundi, Natasha. "Role of Bacteria in Environment." Biotechnology Forums, 2010–2017, Retrieved October 16, 2017. https://www.biotechnologyforums.com/thread-44.html.

Medline Plus. "Over-the-Counter Medicines." August 7, 2017. https://medlineplus.gov/overthecountermedicines.html.

Mela, Sara, BSc, and David E. Whitworth, PhD. "The Fist Bump: A More Hygienic Alternative to the Handshake." *American Journal of Infection Control* 42: 916-917, 2014. http://www.apic.org/Resource_/TinyMceFileManager/Fist_bump_article_AJIC_August_2014.pdf.

Melone, Linda. "10 Germiest Gym Hotspots." *Prevention*, October 15, 2012. http://www.prevention.com/fitness/fitness-tips/where-germs-and-bacteria-lurk-in-your-gym.

The Microbe World. "Shapes of Microbes." Retrieved October 6, 2017. http://www.edu.pe.ca/southernkings/microshapes.htm.

The National Academies. "How Pathogens Make Us Sick." The National Academy of Sciences, 2017. http://needtoknow.nas.edu/id/infection/how-pathogens-make-us-sick.

NHS. "Are We Too Clean for Our Own Good?" July 10, 2015. http://www.nhs.uk/Livewell/homehygiene/Pages/are-we-too-clean-for-our-own-good.aspx.

Perras-Charron, Michelle. "Dirt and Germs: They're Good for Kids." Health & Wellness, February 1, 2017. https://www.baystateparent

.com/2017/02/01/dirt-and-germs-theyre-good-for-kids.

World Health Organization. "Why Is Vaccination Important for Addressing Antibiotic Resistance?" November 2016. http://www .who.int/features/qa/vaccination-antibiotic-resistance/en.

Zyga, Lisa. "We Live in a Bacterial World and It's Affecting Us More Than Previously Thought." Phys.org, February 15, 2013. https://phys.org /news/2013-02-bacterial-world-impacting-previously-thought.html.

INDEX

A

antibiotic resistance, 19, 24, 34–35, 36
antibiotics, 19, 27–28, 35
    in animals, 36
    don't work on viruses, 28
    new, 36
    overuse of, 35–36
antiviral medicine, 28

B

bacteria, 5, 6, 7, 9, 10, 15, 20,
    23, 35
    becoming resistant, 35–36
    on the body, 32
    causing disease, 16, 19, 27, 28
    dangerous, 17, 26
    good, 12, 31, 32–33
    infections, 28
    shapes of, 8
    size of, 10
    where found, 8

C

Centers for Disease Control and
    Prevention (CDC), 35–36
cold virus, 9, 10, 16, 19, 26, 27, 28
colony-forming units (CFUs), 15–16

D

disinfecting, 16, 23, 24–25, 31

E

electron microscope, 8
epidemic, 18

F

fighting disease, 26–29
five-second rule, 22–23
flu virus, 9, 10, 13, 14, 16, 23, 26, 28,
    32
fungal disease, 10

G

genetic material, 7, 8, 9, 26, 28
germaphobe, 4
germs on surfaces, 8, 9, 15–16, 25
grossest places, 16

H

handshake-free zone, 4–6
handwashing, 4, 21–22, 25, 33
healthy habits, 13, 22, 25, 33, 34
how germs spread, 4, 13–14, 15, 18, 20,
    22, 33, 35, 36
how long germs last, 16
human history, 32
hygiene, 22–23, 31, 33, 34
hygiene hypothesis, 30–31, 33

I

immune system, 20, 26–27, 29, 31, 32, 35
infection, 4, 18, 20, 21, 24, 26–27, 29, 36

ABOUT THE AUTHOR

Carol Hand has a PhD in zoology. She has taught college biology, written biology assessments for national assessment companies, written middle and high school science curricula for a national company, and authored numerous young-adult science books, including titles on vaccines, epidemiology, and healthy habits.

PHOTO CREDITS